CW00407062

The
FESTINIOG RAILWAY
FROM 1950

The
FESTINIOG RAILWAY
FROM 1950

Andrew Wilson

TEMPUS

To Joan & Roger Wilson,
Mum and Dad,
who first introduced me
to the delights of the
Festiniog Railway in 1962
and to Tom Davies
whose love of the Railway rubbed off on me.

First published 2002
Copyright © Andrew Wilson, 2002

Tempus Publishing Limited
The Mill, Brimscombe Port,
Stroud, Gloucestershire, GL5 2QG
www.tempus-publishing.com

ISBN 0 7524 2397 5

TYPESETTING AND ORIGINATION BY
Tempus Publishing Limited
PRINTED IN GREAT BRITAIN BY
Midway Colour Print, Wiltshire

Contents

Introduction

Although not the first narrow gauge railway to be built in Wales, the Festiniog Railway is arguably the doyen of its genre. Its origins can be traced back to a meeting between an Englishman, Samuel Holland, who had quarrying interests at Rhiw, and an Irish businessman, Henry Archer, in an inn at Penygroes in December 1829. In 1830 Archer and Holland proposed to link the slate quarries at Ffestiniog with Portmadoc by a railway. James Spooner and Thomas Pritchard surveyed the route aided by James' sons James Swinton and Charles Easton-Spooner. Apart from a pair of inclines over the shoulder of Moelwyn Mawr and the level embankment across the Cob, the line had a continuous falling gradient and could accommodate a gauge of about 2ft, the same as that used in the quarries. This would enable loaded trains to run downhill by gravity while the track bed was wide enough for horses to haul empty wagons uphill and still cope with the sharp curves the topography demanded.

Archer promoted the Bill for the Festiniog Railway, and was successful at the third attempt, the Royal Assent being received on 23 May 1832. The line was opened on 20 April 1836. Despite the economic but rather old-fashioned concept of gravity trains and horse haulage, the railway was able to provide the quarries with an efficient way of transporting their slate to the coast.

The success of the railway was such that the horse and gravity trains became unable to meet the demand of the quarry owners. To avoid delays at the Moelwyn inclines a tunnel was started in December 1839 and was ready for traffic in May 1842. Within a decade the railway was carrying 43,000 tons of slate, a figure that increased to 54,343 tons in 1862. However, this growth was achieved at a cost. One horse could only haul eight empty slate wagons uphill. Consequently for every extra rake of eight slate wagons, an additional horse was required which needed feeding, shoeing and stabling. Consideration was therefore given to conversion to steam traction.

In the 1840s it was generally believed that steam locomotives were an impractical proposition on such a narrow gauge. It was only after Charles Easton-Spooner took control of the railway in 1856 that serious attempts were made to design suitable steam locomotives. This culminated in George England & Co. building four small 0-4-0TTs, *The Princess* and *Mountaineer*, in 1863 and *The Prince* and *Palmerston* the following year. However, the railway was not allowed to carry passengers until 1865.

As traffic increased two slightly larger 0-4-0STTs, *Welsh Pony* and *Little Giant*, were bought in 1867, but the real hindrance to expansion was the single line. In 1869 an Act of Parliament was granted to permit the railway to be doubled. The directors baulked at the costs involved and instead turned to the double engine concept developed by Robert Fairlie, which resulted in *Little Wonder* being delivered in 1869. The locomotive was a revelation, proving to be more than twice as powerful as the 0-4-0TTs.

In 1872 an improved double engine, *James Spooner*, was introduced. In 1873 the railway carried 144,091 tons of slate and returned the empty slate wagons to the Blaenau quarries as well as running a passenger service. A single-bogie Fairlie, *Taliesin*, was introduced in 1876. Two more double engines were built at Boston Lodge works, *Merddin Emrys* in 1879 and *Livingston Thompson* in 1886. In 1873, during this innovative period, carriages 15 and 16 were built. They were the first bogie carriages to run in Britain and they were also the first iron-framed bogie coaches in the world.

The last decades of the nineteenth century saw the Festiniog Railway's near monopoly on the Ffestiniog area's slate traffic challenged by the arrival of standard gauge railways at Minffordd and Blaenau Ffestiniog. As these were able to offer more direct carriage to the inland markets where the slates were required, the halcyon days of the railway were almost over. However, in 1897 the railway still conveyed 139,000 tons of slate. Nevertheless what the standard gauge railways took with one hand they gave back with the other, as tourists were encouraged to travel to Snowdonia and found the Festiniog an irresistible attraction.

Unfortunately the impact of the First World War, allied to changing fashions in roofing materials and a series of strikes, brought the slate industry to its knees and induced what was to prove to be an almost terminal decline. Such was the loss of slate traffic that by the mid-1920s the railway was as dependent on its summer tourist traffic as on its all-year-round slate business. Much was made of the railway's centenary in 1936 by which time the amount of slate carried annually was around 36,000 tons. Posters and timetables encouraged tourists to travel on the Festiniog by advertising the delights of the 'Toy Railway' that ran through the 'wonderland of Wales', thus showing a progressive outlook towards the development of tourist traffic.

Unfortunately these developments were stopped by the outbreak of the Second World War on Sunday 3 September 1939. All passenger trains ceased running on Friday 15 September including the workmen's trains. These were no longer needed because so many of the quarrymen had been conscripted or volunteered. The knock-on effect of this was that slate traffic fell to 12,000 tons a year, and to handle this tonnage the railway began a part-time existence with a skeleton staff of about a dozen. An engine, usually *Princess*, was steamed three times a week to make a single round trip to Blaenau. On the occasions when traffic exceeded *Princess'* capacity *Merddin Emrys* was used. For the first time in 103 years the gravity trains were abandoned.

By the middle of 1945 matters had become dire. Barely 9,000 tons of slate was being transported, mainly because the quarries could no longer rely on the railway. The accumulated backlog of maintenance meant that both rolling stock and permanent way were becoming unreliable. Consequently, when the war ended there was insufficient finance available to even think about restoring the summer passenger service. In fact thoughts turned to closing the railway completely.

By the middle of 1946 the company had decided it could no longer soldier on and decided to close at the start of the quarry holidays. *Princess* was steamed on 1 August and when she returned to Boston Lodge the crew and remaining employees were given notice, except for Robert Evans and Morris Jones, the manager and senior locomotive fitter respectively. There was simply insufficient money to keep the railway running nor, paradoxically, to abandon it as the original Act of Parliament had made no provision for closure. Consequently everything was left where it stood, exposed to vandals, souvenir hunters and more significantly nature and the weather.

The first signs of interest in reviving the Festiniog Railway came in May 1947 when Bill Broadbent surveyed the line and prepared a scheme to restore some services. However, the catalyst to breathe new life into the railway came in 1950 when a schoolboy named Leonard Heath-Humphrys became interested in the Festiniog and made contact with the company regarding the possibility of revival.

Following his first visit to the Festiniog in October 1950, Leonard Heath-Humphrys started a correspondence with Robert Evans, the General Manager, at Portmadoc and Evan Davies, the company's chairman, in London, with a view to re-opening the line with volunteer support. Letters to the railway press elicited support for his ideas and so in September he called a meeting in Bristol to see what could be done to restore the Festiniog. In all thirteen people turned up, including Allan Garraway, who would in time become the railway's General Manager, John Bate, who became the Talyllyn Railway's chief engineer, and Vic Mitchell, who became a Festiniog Railway director.

The problems this group faced were considerable. There was an overdraft at the bank, shareholders had to be negotiated with, if they could be found, and there were legal and technical problems to solve in addition to the railway itself being derelict. Eventually in 1954 Alan Pegler, through his father's good offices, was able to secure a controlling interest in the company for £2,000. So on 24 June 1954 control passed from the old company to Alan Pegler, whose shares were then transferred to a charitable trust, the Festiniog Railway Trust. A volunteer board of directors, supported by a small paid staff and a set of enthusiastic volunteers, were then able to begin the exciting task of restoring the Festiniog Railway to something of its former glory.

Author's Note

I have used the Anglicised form of Festiniog Railway rather than the Welsh Ffestiniog as this is how the name was incorporated and for continuity of the text.

Acknowledgements

I would also like to thank all those people who have helped me with photographs: Adrian Gray, Frank Hornby, Hugh Davies and Desmond Coakham – many thanks, gentlemen. Any errors are mine and mine alone.

One

A Sleeping Giant

When the Festiniog was closed down on 1 August 1946, all the stock not already in Boston Lodge was left where it was standing. At Harbour station, four sidings were full of empty slate wagons parked out of the way as there was insufficient traffic. Boston Lodge works yard was cluttered with the stock of the last passenger train, which had spent much of the war exposed to the elements at Harbour station. The locomotives at least were stored in the engine shed or works. Elsewhere nature had done its best to reclaim the trackbed, especially between Cei Mawr and Tan-y-Bwlch, where lush vegetation all but obscured the track. Above Tan-y-Bwlch the line was eerily complete, a little overgrown but still unmistakably a railway. The photographs in this chapter show the enormity of the task that faced the first volunteers as they struggled to re-open the Festiniog Railway in the early 1950s.

Harbour station on 8 June 1954 with curly roof bogie van No.3 and a box van at the end of a rake of iron slate wagons. The wagon, which can be seen to the right, is an iron coal wagon. In this view the effects of the weather on No.3 are only too apparent; little or no paint, rotten timbers and ivy climbing over the end. (*Desmond Coakham*)

Harbour station again on 8 June 1954 but viewed from a signal post outside the goods shed. Undergrowth now conceals the slate wharfs to the left. The substantial station building and goods shed dating from 1878-1879 have fared much better than rolling stock. In the distance Desmond Coakham has captured on film the harbour and on the far bank more wharfs and slate sheds. *(Desmond Coakham)*

The western end of Boston Lodge works yard on 8 June 1954. Apart from a selection of bogie coaches the cab, tanks and bogie of *Moel Tryfan*, the Welsh Highland Railway's single Fairlie 0-6-4T are visible and on the left hand siding is the Festiniog's unique hearse wagon. As with the previous picture, the main works buildings appear to be sound. *(Desmond Coakham)*

The power bogie and boiler of *Moel Tryfan* were stored in the engine shed awaiting repairs that were never to be undertaken because the locomotive was scrapped to raise badly needed funds. Next to *Moel Tryfan* are the last two locomotives used by the old company, *Merddin Emrys* and *Princess*, in the positions they were stabled back in 1946 in the expectation of further use.

Palmerston was still in Boston Lodges top yard on 28 June 1956. From 1940 to 1946 the engine was used as a stationary boiler to provide steam for the workshop equipment. A further twenty years were to elapse before thoughts turned to restoration with new boiler and cylinders. (*Desmond Coakham*)

This view of Garnedd Tunnel, 18 April 1959, shows the trackbed overgrown but with rails still in place. The section of line above Tan-y-Bwlch was never inundated with trees and was always passable with care. In places the grass was all that kept the rails to gauge. *(R.J. Leonard, courtesy of KRM)*

Half a mile above Garnedd Tunnel, Coed-y-Bleiddiau curve is pictured on 19 March 1961 with the sleepers and chairs just visible. The condition of the track is a testimony to the quality of the pre-war Festiniog's permanent way. *(R.J. Leonard, courtesy of KRM)*

The water tank on Dduallt tank curve is nine miles from Portmadoc and in this view of 19 March 1961 the track is completely hidden. Just behind the photographer's back is the site of Campbell's Platform, built in 1962 to serve Dduallt Manor after restoration by Colonel Campbell. *(R.J. Leonard, courtesy of KRM)*

Dduallt station was one of the most isolated spots on the Festiniog, yet before the First World War it boasted its own stationmaster, Gwilym Deudraeth. Seen on 19 March 1961 the track continues to Moelwyn Tunnel, which by this time had been sealed as the CEGB had built a pumped storage power station near Tan-y-Grisiau whose lower reservoir had flooded the line between Moelwyn Tunnel and Tan-y-Grisiau. *(R.J. Leonard, courtesy of KRM)*

The southern portal of Moelwyn Tunnel on 19 March 1961. The narrow confines of the tunnel were not the most pleasant of places, especially when travelling behind a hard-working engine on an up train. (*R.J. Leonard, courtesy of KRM*)

Duffws, end of the line, seen on 27 April 1959. The station opened for passengers in 1866 and was closed in 1930. The single track leads to the Votty & Bowydd Quarry while another incline branched left to the Maenofferen Quarry. The station buildings are behind the coaches in the car park and are now public toilets. (*R.J. Leonard, courtesy of KRM*)

Two

A New Beginning

With the Festiniog in new hands, a start could be made on bringing it back to life. As a precursor to this, Colonel McMullen of HM Railway Inspectorate visited the whole railway on a typically wet day on 18 August 1954. He was surprised at the neglected state of the railway, especially below Tan-y-Bwlch where trees and rhododendrons smothered the track. The Colonel acknowledged that the trackbed had been well engineered and was sound but he doubted whether a wheel could turn without spending upwards of £40,000. Undaunted, work started at Boston Lodge where Allan Garraway and Bill Harvey succeeded in getting the Simplex tractor working. The starting of the Dorman petrol engine was symbolic as the railway was visibly coming back to life. The pictures in this section illustrate the task facing the small band of volunteers and their achievements.

With the Simplex running, the track leading onto the Cob was dug out from the sand which had buried it, and on 23 September 1954, coupled to coaches Nos 10 and 17, Allan Garraway drove the first train to run on the Festiniog Railway for over eight years. The train made its way to Portmadoc where the petrol tank was replenished. The Festiniog was coming back to life. (F.R. Archives)

By March 1955 the main line had been cleared sufficiently to allow the Simplex to run through to Blaenau Ffestiniog again and trips were made up the line to recover wagons and other reusable items. Here, on 9 April 1956, Allan Garraway and Fred Boughey took their families to Blaenau Ffestiniog to collect a telephone pole for use elsewhere. (*F.R. Archives*)

Sufficient progress had been made for the Portmadoc to Boston Lodge section to re-open in 1955. On 22 July Colonel McMullen made a formal inspection of the line and permitted a passenger service to start the following day. Here the first train, made up of green and ivory-painted carriages Nos 12 and 23 hauled by the Simplex, forms the 2.30 p.m. to Boston Lodge – the first public train on the Festiniog since 1939. (*F.R. Archives*)

The first half of 1955 saw *Prince* re-built under the supervision of Morris Jones and by 3 August 1955 take over the Boston Lodge shuttle, nine years after *Princess* had last run. Here, carrying the Union Jack and Welsh flag, *Prince* backs onto its two-carriage train for its first passenger duty since before 1939. *(F.R. Archives)*

Prince, driven by Allan Garraway, makes a stirring sight as it works the 2.30 p.m. to Boston Lodge on 3 August 1955. From then until September 1956, when *Taliesin* went into traffic, *Prince* worked every passenger train. *(F.R. Archives)*

For the Festiniog Railway Society AGM on 24 March 1956 the unrestored *Merddin Emrys* was taken to Portmadoc with carriages Nos 15, 17, 22, 23 and 12 for display. As can be seen from the state of the track only minor repairs had been carried out. (*F.R. Archives*)

The Cob not only carries the railway between Boston Lodge and Portmadoc but also the main A487 trunk road; note the lack of traffic in 1955. *Prince* has left two carriages at Pen Cob halt and is running towards the works. The rubble in the foreground marks the site of the demolished Second World War pillbox.

19 May 1956 saw services extended to Minffordd and here *Prince* waits at Portmadoc with the 2.00 p.m. service on 22 August 1956. Three carriages, Nos 11, 12 and 17, look smart in their livery of green and ivory with red ends.

On 27 June 1956 *Prince* and coach No.11 were at Minffordd. The station shelter behind *Prince* houses the ticket office and single line token equipment. The track, although clearly visible, is still surrounded by grass and soil. (*Desmond Coakham*)

On 28 June 1956 the Simplex and coach No.11 are at Minffordd awaiting the arrival of a Stephenson Locomotive Society party who were to travel to Boston Lodge. Allan Garraway is seen unlocking the compartment doors, a safety feature unique to the Festiniog to prevent passengers opening the doors in the narrow cuttings, which abound on the line. (*Desmond Coakham*)

Although passenger services only ran as far as Minffordd in 1956, works trains were often seen further up the line. On the evening of 27 June 1956 the Simplex, driven by Allan Garraway, and carriage No.10 are about to run up to Tan-y-Bwlch. The bell at the front was used to warn of the Simplex's approach. (*Desmond Coakham*)

By August 1956 the ex-WD Baldwin 0-4-0 tractor *Moelwyn* had been fitted with a Gardner 3LW diesel engine and is seen in the down loop at Minffordd with a maintenance train made up of carriage No.10 and three wagons bound for Tan-y-Bwlch. (*F.R. Archives*)

Moelwyn had reached Tan-y-Bwlch with the train seen in the previous picture and is stood by the station house. *Moelwyn* was a rough rider as a 0-4-0 and was re-built as a 2-4-0 at the end of 1957. (*F.R. Archives*)

The highlight of 1956 was the return to traffic of the double Fairlie *Taliesin*, the erstwhile *Livingston Thompson*, on 5 September. Here *Taliesin* is over the pit at Boston Lodge and displays the classic lines of a Spooner-inspired double engine.

Seen at Penrhyn station before it was re-opened in 1957 *Moelwyn*, now facing downhill, waits at the throat of the siding with brake van No.1, which had been converted from a quarryman's coach. Penrhyn station was re-built in 1879 using materials from the original Portmadoc station. (*F.R. Archives*)

The 1957 season saw the line reopened as far as Penrhyn, just over three miles from Portmadoc. Four carriages, Nos 11, 12, 17 and 18, were available for traffic and are seen here at Portmadoc on 22 May 1957 forming the 2.00 p.m. to Penrhyn.

Prince has run round at Penrhyn as two passengers record the scene with their cameras. From the station at Penrhyn, high above the village, travellers gain their first glimpse of Harlech Castle some five miles to the south.

The train above has run downhill and is passing Pen Cob halt outside Boston Lodge works. The fireman is on the tender as *Prince*'s small cab was an uncomfortable place for a crew of two. Little firing was needed for the return runs from Penrhyn but the fireman is keeping an eye on the boiler pressure to ensure the vacuum for the brake was maintained.

With the re-opening to Tan-y-Bwlch planned for 1958 it was realised that *Prince* and *Taliesin* would have no back-up if one of them failed. So when the opportunity arose in 1957 to acquire a modern Peckett 0-6-0ST from the closed Harrogate Gasworks railway it was snapped up. Here the powerful looking Peckett is in Boston Lodge yard in company with *Taliesin*. (*R.J. Leonard, courtesy of KRM*)

22 September 1957 witnessed the first steam working beyond Tan-y-Bwlch since 1946, with *Prince* taking carriage No.10 up the line. Strenuous efforts were being made at this time to get the four miles from Penrhyn to Tan-y-Bwlch open for passenger traffic the following year. (*F.R. Archives*)

To the casual observer Tan-y-Bwlch has changed little since 1946 as this view of the station house on 27 March 1958 shows. However, the works train in the up loop, comprising a four-wheel carriage, bogie flat wagon loaded with new sleepers, a bolster and slate wagon, shows that work is in hand to upgrade the track. (*R.J. Leonard, courtesy of KRM*)

The next day the works train had been shunted to allow volunteers to continue with the important business of fettling the up loop. The down loop was less of a priority, as it would only be used as a run-round loop. (*R.J. Leonard, courtesy of KRM*)

From the top end of Tan-y-Bwlch station the rural location of the station is evident. There is still plenty of work to do before the station can welcome its first passengers since 1939. The water tank is leaking and the track still requires attention, principally spot re-sleepering. (*R.J. Leonard, courtesy of KRM*)

Services to Tan-y-Bwlch resumed on 5 April 1958 with *Taliesin* handling the heavier trains. On 15 July 1958 *Taliesin* is at the head of a five carriage train comprising the three restored bowsiders, Nos 17, 18 and 19, with Nos 11 and 12 at the rear. By this time No.12 had been converted to a brake-buffet car and No.11 to an observation car. *(Frank Hornby)*

Taliesin has reached Minffordd and the fireman waits for the train to slow before jumping off and changing the Portmadoc to Minffordd single line token for that between Minffordd and Tan-y-Bwlch. The large tree framing *Taliesin* is believed to have been planted when the railway opened in 1836.

Bessie Jones, in traditional Welsh costume, chats to the crew after *Taliesin* has run round before returning to Portmadoc. Next to the locomotive is the observation car No.11. A first class supplement was charged to travel in the observation saloon, which had been fitted with ex-Mersey Railway seats. (*Frank Hornby*)

After arriving at Portmadoc with a down train, the locomotive would uncouple and take water. *Taliesin* has just done this on 8 July and is about to run over Portmadoc's unique three-way stub point and past the slotted shunting signal. (*Desmond Coakham*)

Taliesin has moved forward to take on coal. The coal bunkers on a double Fairlie took up part of each of the fireman's side water tanks. The sharply curved connection in the foreground leads to the derelict slate yard on the New Wharf. (*Desmond Coakham*)

The first of the bowsiders to be restored to traffic was No.17, which had five third-class and one first-class compartment. The livery is green and ivory with red ends, which suited the fully panelled carriages very well. Unfortunately the livery was time-consuming to apply. (*Desmond Coakham*)

Despite having a fully equipped works, it was not always possible to carry out all the locomotive maintenance under cover. Here fitter, Arwyn Morgan, is replacing *Taliesin*'s buffer beam after re-setting the valves on 31 August 1958.

At the same time a volunteer fitter is replacing *Taliesin*'s big end brasses. The drive to the mechanical lubricator has also been dismantled and the forked connecting rod had been freed from the piston crosshead.

Since powering the re-opening trains across the Cob in 1955 the Simplex tractor has been relegated to less glamorous but equally important tasks such as here, shunting Boston Lodge works yard, on 31 August 1958.

While *Taliesin* was worked on in the open air, four-wheeled brake van No.2, a converted quarryman's coach, receives attention to its roof. The vacuum brake gauge and brake pillar cab just be seen through the open van door, 31 August 1958.

In 1959 the overhaul of the other extant double Fairlie, *Merddin Emrys*, began. Here the boiler and power units devoid of tanks and cab are in the works at Boston Lodge. The basic principals of the Fairlie can be seen – the double-ended boiler with two fireboxes carried on a frame, which is pivoted to the power bogies. (*R.J. Leonard, courtesy of KRM*)

Jim Maxwell has a good head of steam as *Taliesin* leaves Tan-y-Bwlch for Portmadoc in April 1959. The four-wheel carriages in the siding were used to form the 'Flying Flea', an extra service run at peak periods usually behind *Prince*. (*R.J. Leonard, courtesy of KRM*)

Prince in Tan-y-Bwlch cutting with the 'Flying Flea' supplemented by Ashbury bogie carriage No.22 in August 1959. The original long loop used by gravity slate trains has by now been reduced in length, leaving the cutting single track. *(R.J. Leonard, courtesy of KRM)*

Not all of the extant rolling stock was in good enough condition to restore to traffic. One such carriage was Ashbury No.21 seen in Boston Lodge in 1959. It was eventually dismantled and its bogies used under No.26. *(R.J. Leonard, courtesy of KRM)*

Prince heads an up train through the woods at Whistling Curve. This scene has changed considerably since the 1950s as the trees and rhododendrons have all but obscured the track from the lineside.

Prince is leaving Boston Lodge halt for Harbour station. The building to the left is the old engine shed and the photographer is standing where the shed's water tank was located. The narrow clearances are typical of much of the railway's main line.

Three
Consolidation & Expansion

The 1960 season was the sixth since the re-opening of the Festiniog Railway. With Tan-y-Bwlch established as the upper terminus, a period of consolidation followed as track, rolling stock and passenger facilities were improved. During the 1960s the number of passengers carried rose from 102,000 in 1960 to almost 320,000 in 1970. This put considerable pressure on the railway's infrastructure and brought about significant developments in motive power and passenger carriages. The completion of the CEGB's pumped storage power station at Tan-y-Grisiau had flooded the line between Moelwyn Tunnel and Tan-y-Grisiau station. To regain Blaenau Ffestiniog, a deviation was planned at Dduallt to take the railway above the newly created lake, Llyn Ystradau. Work started in 1965 and was advanced sufficiently to permit passenger services to be extended to Dduallt in 1968, the year in which the author first worked as a footplate volunteer on the Festiniog.

In 1962 *Linda* was hired from the Penrhyn Quarry Railway and was followed in 1963 by *Blanche*. Both locomotives were eventually bought and after modifications have become the backbone of the Festiniog's locomotive fleet. In August 1964 *Blanche* waits at Portmadoc with a train for Tan-y-Bwlch.

Although trains had been running to Tan-y-Bwlch since 1958 the track still required a lot of attention to bring it back to pre-1939 standards. On 25 March 1961 re-sleepering of the chaired bullhead track at Two Gates took place. *(R.J. Leonard, courtesy of KRM)*

Some of the cuttings below Tan-y-Bwlch have very limited clearances, just wide enough to permit the passage of a train. Consequently the track and its alignment have to be maintained to the highest possible standards. *(R.J. Leonard, courtesy of KRM)*

The three miles of track below Tan-y-Bwlch is in Forestry Commission land and in dry weather hard-working locomotives throwing out sparks from their chimneys and coals from their ash pans often caused fires. This was to remain a problem, and an insurance expense, until the introduction of oil-firing. *(R.J. Leonard, courtesy of KRM)*

Dduallt station on 19 March 1961, with the isolated house Rhoslyn, presenting a desolate picture. In 1968 this scene was to be transformed, as the railway was re-opened from Tan-y-Bwlch to Dduallt. *(R.J. Leonard, courtesy of KRM)*

With the consent of Buckingham Palace, *Taliesin* was given one of the Duke of Edinburgh's titles and re-named *Earl of Merioneth* at Minffordd during the Festiniog Railway Society's AGM on 22 April 1961. Here the *Earl* is shunting stock at Portmadoc prior to the re-naming ceremony. *(R.J. Leonard, courtesy of KRM)*

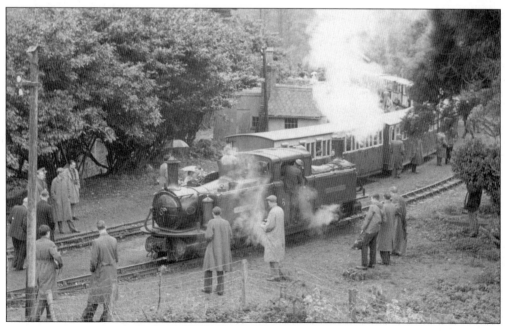

After receiving its new name, *Earl of Merioneth* worked a special society train to Tan-y-Bwlch and is seen running round. The locomotive carried two nameplates, one in English and one in Welsh, plus two Fairlies Patent plates on the tank sides. *(R.J. Leonard, courtesy of KRM)*

The big event of 1961 was the return to steam of the second extant double Fairlie *Merddin Emrys*. The angular shape of the new welded tanks prevented the cab being fitted. The newly restored *Merddin Emrys* is seen being run-in with *Moelwyn*, now running as a 2-4-0, on a short train of four-wheelers on 22 April 1961. *(R.J. Leonard, courtesy of KRM)*

On the same day, *Merddin Emrys* worked its first passenger train. Having reached Tan-y-Bwlch some society members are being given footplate rides. *Merddin Emrys* is running in a red oxide undercoat as there had been insufficient time to paint the locomotive. *(R.J. Leonard, courtesy of KRM)*

The front end of *Earl of Merioneth* displays the classic lines of a Spooner-inspired double engine as it takes on water at Tan-y-Bwlch on AGM day, 1961. *(R.J. Leonard, courtesy of KRM)*

However, the front end of *Merddin Emrys* is very different. The wagon-top boiler, chimney and dome are pure Spooner while the angular water tanks and lack of cab, sand boxes and front footplate give the double engine a very different aspect at Tan-y-Bwlch on AGM day 1961. *(R.J. Leonard, courtesy of KRM)*

The fireman's side of *Merddin Emrys* at Tan-y-Bwlch on AGM day 1961 shows how the coalbunkers are inset into the tanks. There has not been enough time to replace the old style couplings with the chopper type adopted by the new company. The locomotive also lacks vacuum brakes. *(R.J. Leonard, courtesy of KRM)*

Earl of Merioneth and *Merddin Emrys* are at Portmadoc in August 1961. *Merddin Emrys*, seen leaving with a train for Tan-y-Bwlch, has now been fitted with vacuum brakes and chopper couplings. *(R.J. Leonard, courtesy of KRM)*

To ease a locomotive shortage, *Linda* was hired from the Penrhyn Quarry Railway in 1962 and was fully tested to assess her suitability. Running without a tender, *Linda* is in Minffordd yard collecting coal wagons from the interchange sidings. *(F.R. Archives)*

By 1963 *Linda* was in service and running with *Princess*'s old wooden-framed tender, having been fitted with a vacuum ejector and new tyres. Backing into Portmadoc to take the day's first train to Tan-y-Bwlch, Allan Garraway is seen at the regulator having adopted *Linda* as his regular locomotive.

Waiting for *Linda* is a rake of green and ivory liveried carriages headed by one of the bowsiders, so named because of the distinctive profile below the window line.

Boston Lodge on 13 June 1963 with *Moelwyn*, *Prince* and *Merddin Emrys* visible. *Merddin Emrys* been given cab weatherboards and lined green livery. The trackwork in the works has received a lot of attention – compare this view with that on page 10. (*Frank Hornby*)

Prince was re-built before the 1963 season, the most noticeable modification being the new extended frames. Modifications were also made to the draughting, which improved *Prince*'s steaming. A full re-paint in standard green edged with black and lined out in red was applied. Here the smokebox is being emptied in Boston Lodge yard on 13 June 1963. *(Frank Hornby)*

1963 marked the centenary of steam traction on the Festiniog Railway. As part of the celebrations, No.1 *Princess* was tidied up and put on display at Harbour station. Coupled to a small wooden framed tender she makes an interesting comparison with the re-built *Prince*. *(Frank Hornby)*

By 1964 the track at Harbour station had been re-modelled. The three-way stub point had been lifted and moved to Glan-y-Mor yard at Boston Lodge on 1 March. The water tank and coal stage are now next to each other and make an interesting comparison with pages 38-39.

The Cob now features a well-maintained track and the three-armed signal still protects Harbour station. On a clear day the footpath alongside the track offers breathtaking views of Snowdon as well as of the trains.

The opposite view along the Cob is dominated by Boston Lodge works with the long shed and erecting shops to the right and the white Boston Lodge cottages are to the left. The cottages were originally the barracks and stables when horses worked the line.

The entrance to the works was also re-modelled to provide a head shunt. To the right is the long engine shed, the erecting shops are behind, and just visible are Boston Lodge Cottages where, at No.1, lived Bill Hoole, the Kings Cross shed top link driver who retired to work on the Festiniog.

Prince has arrived at Tan-y-Bwlch during centenary year. The station still retains much of its pre-preservation charm.

Over the winter of 1963-1964 *Linda* was overhauled and emerged coupled to a re-built tender in lined green livery. Seen taking water at Tan-y-Bwlch, the small cylindrical sand pots have been replaced with larger ones profiled to match the saddle tank.

The fireman's side of *Linda* shows the polished pipework of the injector. The polished dome sets off the green livery to good effect as teenage author and his father intently study the footplate at Portmadoc.

With the fireman working hard, *Merddin Emrys* passes Rhiw Goch with a Tan-y-Bwlch working. The first two carriages are bowsiders and the third is the re-built *Snapper Bar*, the ex-Lynton & Barnstaple buffet car.

Merddin Emrys waits to leave Tan-y-Bwlch for Portmadoc. The train is made up of the same rake of carriages seen on page 50. The addition of weatherboards and sand pots has given the locomotive more of the look of a Spooner Fairlie.

After *Blanche* was overhauled she returned to service in 1965 with a purpose-built tender cab, but did not receive lined green livery until the winter of 1965-1966. Seen at Minffordd on a down train, *Blanche*'s appearance makes an interesting comparison with *Linda*'s on page 47.

In 1966 the opportunity arose to acquire the first Beyer Garratt K1. After raising the £1,000 asking price and another £400 to cover transport, the 0-4-0+0-4-0 arrived at Portmadoc and was put on display at Harbour station where it dwarfed the railway's original rolling stock.

Merddin Emrys brings an afternoon train from Tan-y-Bwlch into Portmadoc. The three carriages next to the locomotive are Nos 100, 14 and 104. No.14 is the re-built ex-Lynton & Barnstaple buffet car while No.100 is the 1965-built Centenary observation car and No.104 is the prototype saloon carriage, soon known as 'barns' because of their size.

A busy time at Portmadoc as *Prince* shunts carriages while *Merddin Emrys* waits on road No.3. The open cab had some advantages but very few on wet days when both driver and fireman needed to don waterproofs. *(R.J. Leonard, courtesy of KRM)*

By the mid-1960s, having been cannibalised to keep *Prince* in traffic, *Palmerston* had been reduced to little more than a rusting hulk hidden away in Glan-y-Mor yard. Even the wildest dreamer at this time would not have considered *Palmerston* as worthy of restoration.

The rest of the railway's unrestored locomotives were at least covered by tarpaulins. Here the Harrogate Peckett, *Welsh Pony*, *Princess*, K1, the ex-BR tamper and carriage No.10 are tucked away behind the long shed.

With the growing fleet of passenger carriages, an extension was added to the carriage shed. The Royal Engineers erected the frame in March 1964 and in this view from 1968 the new roof dominates Boston Lodge as *Prince* passes with an up train.

In 1963 the 3.00 p.m. non-stop train was given the name *Y Cymro* (*The Welshman*). In the mid-1960s *Prince* is waiting to depart with this working from Portmadoc while *Linda* waits on the adjoining line. *Prince*'s driver is Bill Hoole.

In October 1967 a First World War Alco 2-6-2T arrived on the railway from the Tramway de Pithiviers in France. After running trials, it was stripped down for overhaul before entering traffic as *Mountaineer*. It is seen here in July 1968 before rebuilding started.

On 6 April 1968 passenger services extended to Dduallt. As the run-round loop was incomplete, a pilot engine was stationed at Dduallt to release the train engine. *Prince* is seen on the first working about to couple up for the down trip. *(F.R. Archives)*

The summer of 1968 saw only one double engine, *Earl of Merioneth*, in traffic, as *Merddin Emrys* had been withdrawn in need of a new boiler. *Earl of Merioneth* catches the early evening sun over the locomotive pit at Boston Lodge.

The end of the line at Portmadoc in July 1968. *Linda* simmers in late summer sunshine as developers irrevocably change the backdrop of the New Wharf.

Blanche wheels a down train away from Boston Lodge halt on the last leg of its journey to Portmadoc. The building on the left is the old company's engine shed, which by 1968 was used to store vehicles out of traffic.

Linda heads an up train of Centenary stock past the lay-by at Rhiw Plas Bridge in July 1968. The General Manager, Allan Garraway, is in his customary position when driving *Linda*. The clear exhaust and lack of steam at the safety valves shows that the fireman is on top of his job.

Between Minffordd and Penrhyn the railway runs along a straight embankment, Gwyndy Bank. *Linda* is seen climbing Gwyndy Bank with an up train in July 1968. The four-wheel carriage behind the tender was built by the Midland Group of the Festioniog Railway Society on the frames of an ex-quarryman's coach.

An evening train was run in the late 1960s which was frequented by many of the volunteers working on the railway, who tended to occupy the licensed buffet car. In late July 1968 *Prince* restarts the last train of the day from Penrhyn.

Linda cautiously eases an up train over the level crossing at Penrhyn. At this time, July 1968, the railway crossed two level crossings, excluding the one to Minffordd yard – Lottie's Crossing near Minffordd and this one at Penrhyn.

Linda, in charge of a late afternoon down train, coasts over the iron bridge spanning the B4410 in July 1968. The crew are in typical pose for a down run, the fireman in the tender and Allan Garraway keeping an eye on the track ahead.

Immediately after crossing Tan-y-Bwlch Bridge, up trains enter Tan-y-Bwlch cutting. *Prince* is still working hard and the driver will not shut off steam until arrival at the station. The scorching of *Prince*'s smokebox is evidence of how hard the 1863 veteran has to work to keep time with the loads in 1968.

By the summer of 1968 the Festiniog's passenger stock was running in a mixture of liveries. Bowsider No.19 is still in green, ivory and red, standardised in 1955.

The green and cream livery was attractive but time-consuming to apply and so, with the introduction of the Centenary stock, it was decided to re-paint all the passenger-carrying vehicles in varnished teak. Here Nos 22 and 23 are seen at Portmadoc in this livery.

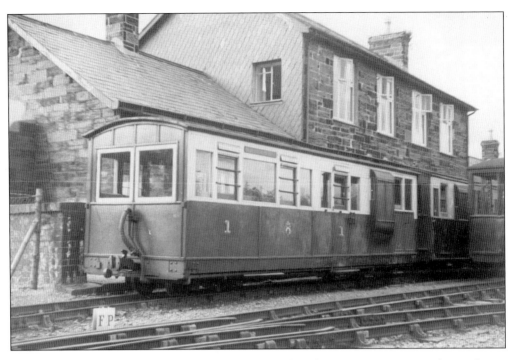

Observation car No.11 and buffet car No.12 are still in the attractive green and ivory livery at Portmadoc.

Centenary stock observation car No.100 at Portmadoc in July 1968 shows how the varnished teak livery weathered at different rates giving an uneven finish to the side panels.

Four

On to Dduallt
and Tan-y-Grisiau

The 1970s were an exciting time for the Festiniog Railway as work continued on the deviation around Llyn Ystradau. In 1971 the Lands Tribunal awarded the railway £100,000, plus interest, for loss of earnings over the flooded part of the line. Although not enough to reinstate the route, it was enough to build a new tunnel. Work started on the tunnel in 1972 and by the end of 1976 the basic tunnel was complete. In 1977 services were extended through the tunnel to Llyn Ystradau and to Tan-y-Grisiau in 1978. The early years of the decade saw the steam locomotives converted to oil-firing. More new coaches were built as passenger journey figures rose to 409,693 in 1978. The following year a brand new double Fairlie, built at Boston Lodge, was put into traffic.

The only double Fairlie to work throughout the 1970s was *Merddin Emrys*, seen here running into Tan-y-Bwlch on 15 August 1979. Having received a new parallel boiler in 1969-1970, *Merddin Emrys* was converted to oil-firing in the winter of 1972-1973.

In 1969 *Princess* was put on display near the council offices at Blaenau Ffestiniog as a token of good faith that the railway would re-open to the town. No.1 was still on display in 1970.

Prince had been taken out of traffic for overhaul in 1968. As the locomotive had limited haulage powers, it had a low priority and work did not begin until 1976. Here the cab and saddle tank are seen stored in Glan-y-Mor yard, Boston Lodge.

By 1970 *Earl of Merioneth*'s boiler was coming to the end of its working life and the power bogies were also in need of overhaul. In August 1970 the locomotive, wreathed in steam, is seen entering Tan-y-Bwlch with an up working.

Returning from Dduallt *Earl of Merioneth* drifts into Tan-y-Bwlch. When finally withdrawn on 31 October 1971 the locomotive had run 45,006 miles since 1956. It was decided to preserve the locomotive as *Livingston Thompson* but use the power bogies under a new locomotive, which would perpetuate the *Earl of Merioneth* name.

When returned to traffic in 1970 after a heavy overhaul *Linda* appeared as a 2-4-0ST. The pony truck was fitted to improve *Linda*'s riding, the axle coming from *Moel Tryfan*'s bogie. *Linda* was also converted to oil-firing at the same time.

Mountaineer entered traffic in 1969 and after some teething problems become a reliable performer, albeit at the expense of heavy coal consumption. The new side-window cab makes full use of the loading gauge. The livery of the coaches has changed; the teak finish weathered badly and was replaced by a deep cherry red. The third and fourth coaches are the two tourist coaches built in 1971-1972 to provide extra fine weather capacity. September 1972.

At times when traffic was very heavy or when a steam locomotive failed, *Moelwyn* could be found on passenger duties. On 15 September 1970 *Moelwyn* heads the 4.00 p.m. down relief from Dduallt towards Penrhyn crossing.

Merddin Emrys is seen running into Tan-y-Bwlch in September 1970. Fitted with a new boiler, no dome covers and still coal-fired, the double Fairlie's appearance is austere in comparison with the traditional Spooner look seen on page 63.

After being superheated and converted to oil-firing, it was discovered that the black paint on *Linda*'s smokebox became badly burnt. Until a more heat resistant black paint could be sourced, the smokebox was painted with aluminium paint as seen here at Portmadoc.

Blanche was converted to oil-firing in 1971 and this view of her on 6 September 1971 at Portmadoc on the 1.15 p.m. departure for Dduallt makes a very interesting comparison with that above of *Linda*.

Coasting to a halt at Minffordd in September 1970, the re-boilered *Merddin Emrys* is the pragmatic solution to keeping at least one double engine in traffic when the railway's major aim was to re-open to Blaenau Ffestiniog.

In 1974 building work started at Harbour station to enlarge the shop and buffet. Behind *Blanche* the steel framework is complete and work has begun on the walls and windows.

After leaving Boston Lodge halt the line runs above the A487 on an embankment to Rhiw Plas. *Merddin Emrys* effortlessly lifts its train along this section with just a feather of steam at the safety valve.

Mountaineer's boiler had fairly large tubes, which reduced the boiler's efficiency when working hard, thus making steam-raising somewhat problematic. Running into Minffordd, *Mountaineer's* fireman is setting the injector to get some water into the boiler.

Unusually *Mountaineer*'s tanks are topped up at the small water tank at Minffordd. The fireman has the blower on as well as the injector to ensure there is enough steam to get to Penrhyn.

What a Fairlie is all about! *Merddin Emrys* is seen making light work of a train comprising three four-wheel coaches and ten bogies on Gwyndy Bank.

In an attempt to prevent *Mountaineer*'s fire-throwing characteristic, a spark arrestor was fitted to the chimney in 1971. *Mountaineer* is seen at Penrhyn in this form.

In the early 1970s the passing loop at Penrhyn was upgraded to allow passenger trains to pass. A down train waits as *Linda* brings an up train. Unusually for a Festiniog station the up train is using the left hand track; normally up workings used the right hand side of loops.

Normally *Linda* and *Blanche* were limited to seven or eight bogie coaches but on heavier trains a pilot would be taken. *Moelwyn* is double heading *Blanche* into Tan-y-Bwlch in September 1971 with a heavy Dduallt-bound working. In the siding is the Simplex, by now named *Mary Ann*, with a permanent-way train.

In 1970 *Moelwyn* with quarryman's coach No.8, four-wheel coaches Nos 5 and 6, plus brake vans Nos 1 and 2, worked a shuttle service between Tan-y-Bwlch and Dduallt known as the Dduallt Diddy. *Moelwyn* receives a little sprucing up after arrival at Tan-y-Bwlch.

Early and late in the season the weather at Tan-y-Bwlch can sometimes be described as Welsh mist. In just such conditions *Mountaineer* runs through the platform to draw up by the water tank to replenish her tanks.

Between Tan-y-Bwlch and Garnedd Tunnel the railway runs along a shelf high above Llyn Mair and the B4410. *Linda* heads a down working along this stretch to Tan-y-Bwlch.

By the time *Linda* arrives at Dduallt in August 1972, the pre-stressed concrete bridge to carry the deviation over the old line had been built. Rhoslyn Bridge was named after the house and lake next to the station (see page 37).

To provide the run-round loop at Dduallt the rocky hillside had to be trimmed, a job completed by two Blaenau quarrymen. *Earl of Merioneth* is pictured on the loop.

Behind *Linda* can be seen the line of the deviation at Barn site, still climbing and curving round to parallel the old route towards Moelwyn Bach. It is a sobering thought that volunteer labourers constructed the embankments of the deviation.

Dduallt's isolation is interrupted by *Merddin Emrys*'s preparation to depart. Driver Evan Davies is oiling round and checking the bearings. Rhoslyn is virtually hidden by the trees behind the locomotive.

In 1975 a shuttle service was run over the completed section of the deviation. *Moel Hebog* and coach No.110, the railway's first steel-clad passenger carriage, wait for passengers.

Seen from the Dduallt shuttle is the deviation mess, built on the alignment of the original route at the entrance of Moelwyn Tunnel. This view gives a clear indication of the height of the new route and the reason for the construction of the spiral at Dduallt.

When Dduallt is used as a passing place, it is possible to see up and down trains at Rhoslyn Bridge. The Planet diesel *Upnor Castle* heads an up working as *Linda* coasts over the bridge in charge of a down working.

A water tank was provided at Dduallt. *Blanche* is now a 2-4-0ST oil-fired and has been fitted with new fabricated piston valve cylinders. When the line to Llyn Ystradau was opened in 1977, Dduallt was signalled to allow passenger trains to pass each other here.

A station was opened at Llyn Ystradau in the summer of 1977, solely comprising a run-round loop and head shunt. The temporary nature of the station is apparent as *Blanche* runs round on the unballasted loop.

To the left of *Blanche* is Llyn Ystradau itself and beyond the points the main line runs towards the new Moelwyn Tunnel.

Dduallt became a passing place with the opening of the line through to Llyn Ystradau. *Merddin Emrys* brings a down train off the spiral with the foothills of Moel Ystradau dominating the view.

The curvature of the spiral is apparent as *Linda* wheels a down trains into Dduallt and passes *Mountaineer* on an up train. The up train will pass through 360 degrees and, in so doing, cross over the up main line and run through the woods above *Mountaineer*'s cab.

Llyn Ystradau station was only meant to be a temporary stepping-stone before Tan-y-Grisiau was opened. The second of two inaugural trains headed by *Blanche* and *Merddin Emrys* approaches the Afon Cwmorthin Bridge on 24 June 1978. *(F.R. Archives)*

Like Tan-y-Bwlch station, that at Tan-y-Grisiau was built on a curve. *Merddin Emrys* leaves Tan-y-Grisiau with a Portmadoc-bound train. Note that the track here is of a much more substantial flat-bottomed variety secured by clips.

With the opening of Tan-y-Grisiau station trains ran above but parallel to Lyn Ystradau. *Linda* wheels a down train over this section heading for the new Moelwyn Tunnel.

Mountaineer has passed the new summit behind the power station with a down working. One of the possible deviation routes had been to run along the opposite side of the lake and along the top of the dam in the background.

Mountaineer brings a train, comprised of a single bowsider and modern stock, into Tan-y-Grisiau. The station is dominated by the flanks of Ceseiliau Moelwyn down, which cascades the Afon Cwnmorthin.

Linda is in charge of a Portmadoc train crossing the Afon Cwnmorthin Bridge at Tan-y-Bwlch. The river tumbles down the hillside creating a waterfall just above the bridge.

When trains started to run to Tan-y-Grisiau, a water tank was built and temporary toilets provided for the public. *Mountaineer* is seen replenishing its tanks in the summer of 1979.

The points at the top end of Tan-y-Grisiau station mark the place where the deviation rejoins the old route to Blaenau Ffestiniog. *Mountaineer* is about to cross these points to complete running round its train.

Between Moelwyn Tunnel and Tan-y-Grisiau the line runs above Llyn Ystradau to a new summit behind the power station. *Linda* is on the last stretch towards the power station summit.

The deviation line with its new summit meant that the Festiniog could no longer boast a continual downhill gradient from Blaenau to Portmadoc. *Linda* is climbing through summit cutting with a down train.

1979 was not only notable for the re-opening of Tan-y-Grisiau station but also for the introduction of a brand-new double Fairlie, *Earl of Merioneth/Iarll Meirionydd*, designed to be capable of working through to Blaenau Ffestiniog without needing to take one water. It is seen here shunting at Portmadoc.

The slab-sided *Earl of Merioneth/Iarll Meirionydd* is heading an up train across the Cob. Many Festiniog purists were unhappy about the functional appearance of the new Fairlie. The reader can judge for themselves and make up their own minds.

While much effort was expended to get back to Blaenau Ffestiniog *Prince* was also restored to traffic in 1980 with a superheated boiler. Resplendent in standard FR green-lined livery, the 117-year-old veteran is seen above at Boston Lodge.

Mountaineer, running bunker first across the Cob, was still proving a hard-working and reliable locomotive. Its symmetrical wheel arrangement was easier on the track than *Linda* and *Blanche*.

The privately-owned Hunslet quarry locomotive, *Britomart*, is raising steam at Boston Lodge. The 0-4-0ST is the smallest steam engine on the Festiniog and is used occasionally on light works trains. At present *Britomart* is dismantled for a heavy overhaul.

Earl of Merioneth/Iarll Meirionydd, however, could handle the heaviest trains and is seen here with a heavy summer working leaving Tan-y-Bwlch.

Five
The Final Goal –
Blaenau Ffestiniog

In 1954 the goal of the pioneer preservationists had been to restore the Festiniog Railway between Portmadoc and Blaenau Ffestiniog. By 1979 less than two miles of track remained to be re-opened, all on the old alignment between Tan-y-Grisiau and Blaenau Ffestiniog. It was to take three more years to upgrade the trackbed, repair damaged retaining walls and restore bridges and culverts before that goal was achieved on 25 May 1982, almost twenty-seven years after the Simplex tractor worked the new company's first train on 23 July 1955. The station at Blaenau Ffestiniog was designed as a British Rail/Festiniog interchange on the site of the Great Western/Festiniog station of 1883.

Snow caps Manod Mawr as *Earl of Merioneth/Iarll Meirionydd* runs round at Blaenau Ffestiniog as a British Rail diesel multiple unit arrives from Llandudno Junction and the Conway Valley line. The standard gauge line continued along the trackbed of the former line to Bala as far as Trawsfyndd where it served the nuclear power station.

With the weather doing its best to hinder work, the first steam train to Glan-y-Pwll arrived on 11 December 1981 behind *Blanche* and *Moelwyn*. *(F.R. Archives)*

Blanche's works train arrived at Glan-y-Pwll during a period of atrocious weather. The front buffer beam has proved useful as a snow plough.

24 May 1981 was the day when, for the first time since 1957, the track of the Festiniog railway was continuous from Portmadoc to Glan-y-Pwll. British Rail opened its part of Blaenau Ffestiniog station on 22 March 1982 and to mark the occasion *Blanche* worked a short train into the station alongside the Conway Valley diesel unit. (*F.R. Archives*)

With the Conway Valley unit stabled in the loop, a Class 40 appeared on the nuclear flask working from Trawfynydd power station, providing the unusual sight of three trains at Blaenau Ffestiniog. (*F.R. Archives*)

The Festiniog station was opened to traffic on 25 May 1982, the 150th Anniversary, almost to the day, of the Festiniog's Company's first Act of Parliament. The official opening by The Rt Hon. George Thomas MP, then Speaker of the House of Commons, came on 30 April 1983. Here *Blanche* runs round on the immaculate track at Blaenau Ffestiniog.

Seen from the footbridge linking the standard gauge and narrow gauge sides of the station at Blaenau Ffestiniog, *Earl of Merioneth/Iarll Meirionydd* runs round its track.

It is interesting to look at the developments that have occurred at Blaenau Ffestiniog in the twenty years since re-opening. *Earl of Merioneth/Iarll Meirionydd*, with brass dome covers, runs parallel to the standard gauge tracks with a heavy train in a mixture of liveries in May 1997.

It is now 2000 and the station has a mature look with a purpose-built amenity block and canopy, a much needed feature at one of the British Isles' wettest locations. A second track has been laid so that two trains can be at the top terminus at the same time.

The view towards Glan-y-Pwll shows the new colour light signalling required to control the expanded track layout at Blaenau Ffestiniog.

Main line trains still run alongside those of the Festiniog at Blaenau Ffestiniog as here on a late August evening in 2000 as *Blanche* runs round a Steam & Cuisine working.

Six

The Premier
Narrow Gauge Railway

Although the goal of re-opening to Blaenau Ffestiniog was achieved twenty years ago, in 1982, the Festiniog Railway can justly be regarded as the premier narrow gauge railway in Great Britain. stations, track and rolling stock have all benefited from an ongoing programme of improvements. Significantly the railway's heritage has not been forgotten but retains a high profile, thanks to the efforts of the Heritage Group. In the 1990s Boston Lodge works built two new Fairlies, a double and single engine, with a replica Lynton & Barnstaple 2-6-2T taking shape. The permanent way department has its own dedicated work train and the Welsh Highland Railway has been brought back to life. Galas and special events help keep the railway's profile high and although passenger figures are not as high as in the 1970s the railway's core business is in a healthy state.

A classic Festiniog scene, the 1999-built single Fairlie *Taliesin* takes water at Tan-y-Bwlch during the August 2001 Fairlie Traditional Weekend. *Taliesin's* power bogie is interchangeable with the double Fairlies, bringing some standardisation to the motive power.

In 1984 *Welsh Pony* was put on display at the entrance to Harbour station. The only surviving large England 0-4-0STT, it is to hoped that one day *Welsh Pony* will be restored to traffic.

Prince is more often than not restricted to working the vintage train and Minffordd shuttles. During the 1995 VE Day gala *Prince* is at Minffordd with the shuttle working to Minffordd Yard. The red livery has been carried since 1986.

During the 1999 Vintage Gala *Palmerston* makes a brisk start from Portmadoc with a Vintage Train for Minffordd. *Palmerston* was restored to traffic in 1993, a feat many thought impossible in 1968 (see page 51), and carries lined maroon livery.

Prince was overhauled and re-painted in time for the October 1999 Gala. The appearance of the tender has been improved by rationalising the tender oil tanks. The livery is now lined red.

The extended smokebox betrays the fact that *Prince* has been superheated. The cover on the chimney is to retain smokebox and boiler heat to keep cooling stresses to a minimum.

As *Palmerston* is coal-fired, it is usually confined to working below Rhiw Goch. Seen working a demonstration freight at Minffordd in October 1999 this view makes an interesting comparison with that of *Prince* above.

The VE Day Gala in May 1995 finds two double Fairlies at Portmadoc. The 1992-built *David Lloyd George* is on the left and on the right is *Merddin Emrys*. In 1988 *Merddin Emrys* emerged after a heavy re-build to vintage appearance in lined maroon livery.

Appearances can be deceptive as the Funkey diesel *Vale of Ffestiniog* was built in 1967 while *David Lloyd George*, the steam locomotive, was built in 1992. Both are built to Robert Fairlie's concept of a locomotive with two power bogies.

After withdrawal in October 1971 the boiler and tanks of *Earl of Merioneth* were stored. In 1987 it was decided to restore the locomotive to as near its original appearance as possible and in 1988 it was loaned to the National Railway Museum at York for display as *Livingston Thompson*.

Despite attempts to soften the 1979 *Earl of Merioneth/Iarll Meirionydd* the locomotive still retains its appearance of 'austerity'. Nevertheless the *Iarll* is an effective motive power unit and is seen here being prepared for service at Boston Lodge on 18 August 2001.

Seen through the windows of the push-pull driving trailer, *Earl of Merioneth/Iarll Meirionydd* takes on water at Blaenau Ffestiniog May 1997.

David Lloyd George waits at Minffordd with an up working. Minffordd is the interchange station with the Cambrian Coast Line. It is interesting to compare this view with that on page 27.

David Lloyd George is accelerating up Gwyndy Bank on 6 August 1996 with a heavy afternoon train. The first four coaches are all of different designs and carry varied liveries, a far cry from the 1950s.

On the same day *Earl of Merioneth/Iarll Meirionydd* is running down Gwyndy Bank. The first six coaches in the push-pull set are in green and cream livery while the remaining stock is in the maroon and cream livery first used on the *Mountain Prince*.

The brand new single Fairlie *Taliesin* runs into Portmadoc on 1 May 1999 for the official naming ceremony. Running in plain black, the money to build Taliesin was raised by a covenant scheme.

A little more than two years later *Taliesin*, now running in fully lined out maroon, runs into Minffordd with a Vintage Train on 18 August 2001.

In 1991 *Linda* was re-painted in lined midnight blue. This elegant livery suited the ex-Penrhyn locomotive well as is seen in this 1995 view of her rolling a down train towards Minffordd.

Linda receives some last minute attention at Boston Lodge before taking up her rostered duty. The midnight blue livery can be picked out in monochrome pictures, as the lining is white.

As the fireman checks that all is well with the following train, *Blanche* leaves Portmadoc in October 1996 for Blaenau Ffestiniog.

Blanche is the only Festiniog Railway steam locomotive to remain in its 1960s green livery and is pictured here waiting to leave Tan-y-Bwlch on 6 August 1996

Linda was returned to traffic in October 1996, without her tender, in as near ex-Penrhyn condition as is now possible and running as an oil-burning 2-4-0ST. Seen here raising steam at Boston Lodge on 26 October, *Linda* had to run coupled to *Prince* in order to share a common fuel tank.

Later on the same day *Linda* is double heading an up train with *Prince* across the Cob. *Linda* is now painted in Penrhyn livery. The lining is quite different to the previous midnight blue livery (see page 102).

Mountaineer was turned out in War Department livery as No.1265 for the VE Day Gala in 1995. The Alco is now running with a re-profiled cab which follows the Fairlie pattern; this was to give the crews a better safety envelope when looking out of the cab.

Mountaineer and *Blanche* bring an eleven-coach train across the Cob. *Mountaineer* makes good use of the Festiniog's loading gauge as she almost dwarfs the Hunslet 2-4-0ST.

During the 1995 May Gala *Mountaineer* and *Blanche* work across the Cob. The whistle board is an original Festiniog disc signal, which has been put to a new use.

For the VE Day Gala *Mountaineer* was joined by another ex-WD, Alco No.57148 from Chemin de Fer Touristique Froissy-Cappy-Dompierre. The comparison between the much modified Festiniog locomotive and the almost original condition of the visitor is interesting.

Mountaineer's next livery change was to black lined in red, with the red backed nameplates restored to the tank sides. The illusion of a double chimney is created by the vacuum ejector pipe being sited behind the chimney.

During the Autumn 1999 Gala, the opportunity was taken to recreate some scenes from the Festiniog's past. Here the newly painted *Talisein* rubs shoulder with *David Lloyd George* and *Palmerston* outside the original engine shed at Boston Lodge.

The Festiniog runs a very successful guest driver programme where members of the public can have a day firing and driving a steam locomotive. In September 1997 the author and Neil McMaster are discussing *Linda*'s finer points at Blaenau Ffestiniog.

Later in the day the same guest crew pose with *Linda* at Barn on the deviation just above Dduallt.

Taliesin has also been used on the guest driver programme. In March 2000 the single Fairlie is at Tan-y-Bwlch with the three-coach set of carriages used on these occasions.

The guest driver programme includes helping with preparing the locomotive and disposal duties at the end of the day. Disposal includes running light engine across the Cob to replenish the fuel tank ready for the locomotive's next duty. The fuel oil is taken from the oil tankers in the siding at Harbour station.

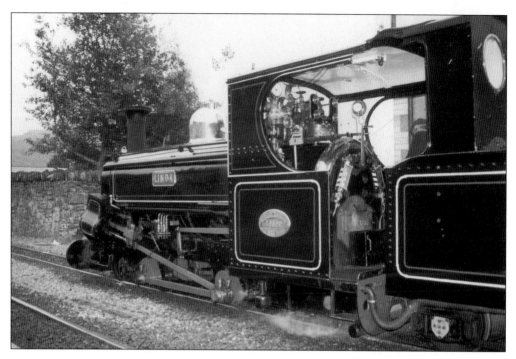

In association with the Maes-y-Nueadd hotel at Talsarnau, the Festiniog runs a series of Steam and Cuisine dining trains throughout the summer. *Linda* is seen here at Blaenau Ffestiniog on one such working in August 1999.

Almost a year to the day later it is *Blanche* this time in charge of a Steam and Cuisine train at Blaenau Ffestiniog.

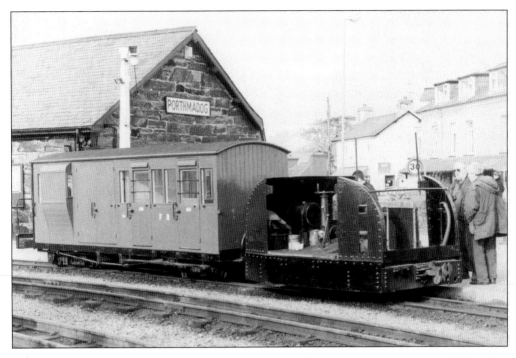

The railway operates a fleet of diesel locomotives of differing age and power. On 26 October 1996 the Simplex tractor and coach No.10 re-enacted one of the early track clearance trains run in 1954-1955. No.10 was re-built and re-entered traffic in 1991.

Moelwyn has also been the recipient of much attention and was recently restored to traffic and is pictured carriage shunting at Boston Lodge in March 2000.

For many years *Upnor Castle* was used as the passenger stand-by diesel (see page 76). With the acquisition of more powerful diesels *Upnor Castle* was kept for less demanding duties except in emergencies.

One such emergency occurred on 6 August 1996 when *David Lloyd George* became a partial failure and needed assistance. The pair are seen at Tan-y-Bwlch preparing to leave for Blaenau Ffestiniog.

A second Planet diesel was acquired and entered traffic on 29 December 1985. Named *Conway Castle* the locomotive was fitted for push-pull operation and painted in the green and ivory livery adopted for the push-pull train. *Conway Castle* is seen leaving Portmadoc with a push-pull working in May 1995.

Another view of *Conway Castle* in push-pull mode in May 1995. Like all the later acquisitions the cab makes full use of the loading gauge clearances. The location is Boston Lodge Curve.

A Baguley-Drewry 0-6-0 diesel-hydraulic was acquired in exchange for the ex-Harrogate Peckett (page 24). Named *Criccieth Castle* this locomotive was also fitted with push-pull control equipment and painted in green and ivory livery. *Criccieth Castle* is entering Portmadoc with a down passenger train on 6 August 1996.

After arriving with a down passenger train, *Criccieth Castle* is shunting carriages for the next up working on 6 August 1996.

114

When the opportunity arose to acquire another Baguley-Drewry 0-6-0 diesel-hydraulic, the locomotive was named *Harlech Castle* and dedicated to the permanent way department. It is seen here in its light grey and yellow PW livery with matching bogie coach at Minffordd on 22 October 2001.

The re-building of a 1967-built Funkey diesel gave the Festiniog what it had long needed – a powerful main line bogie diesel. Put into traffic in 1998 and named *Vale of Ffestiniog*, the locomotive makes an impressive sight at Minffordd on 22 October 2001.

The railway also has a Matisa ballast tamper which was acquired in 1968 and put into traffic in 1977. Named *Stefcomatic* the tamper is seen in action at Harbour station at Easter 2001.

While the tamper was at work *Vale of Ffestiniog* arrived with a down train. They make an interesting comparison at Portmadoc as *Vale of Ffestiniog* waits with the next up working.

Another ex-Penrhyn Quarry locomotive has found a home on the Festiniog. *Lilla* is pictured at Boston Lodge and finds employment on footplate ride and slate shunt duties.

Sgt Murphy, a Kerr Stuart 0-6-2T, was owned by Gordon Rushton, the Festiniog's one-time General Manager. *Sgt Murphy* is crossing the Cob with *Palmerston* during the VE Day Gala.

At the other end of the train seen at the bottom of page 117 were Alco No.57148 and a German WD Feldbahn 0-8-0T CFVO No.6 *Burgonde*. The locomotives were rostered to share the Minffordd shuttles.

Other locomotives to pay working visits to the Festiniog have been *Cloister* and *Bronllwyd*, seen here at Boston Lodge raising steam in the company of *Earl of Merioneth/Iarll Meirionydd* .

For the Penrhyn Gala in October 1996 *Linda* was joined by *Lilla*, *Lilian* and *George Sholto*. The latter three are lined here at Portmadoc.

Some much smaller guests have starred at galas. The Leighton Buzzard's de Winton 0-4-0VB *Challoner* is seen in company of the even smaller Groudle Glen 2-4-0T *Sea Lion* from the Isle of Man.

Challoner and *Lilla* shunt slate wagons at Minffordd. The line in the foreground descends to the bottom yard and erstwhile exchange sidings (see page 42).

Ex-SAR NGG16 2-6-2+2-6-2 Garratt No.138 is in steam at Glan-y-Pwll on 3 May 1997. The locomotive destined for the Welsh Highland Railway had been overhauled and painted dark green. The PW Department's *Moel Hebog* is outside the carriage shed and makes an interesting comparison with the picture on page 75.

Also on display at Gal-y-Pwll on 3 May 1997 was another Garratt destined for the Welsh Highland Railway, ex-SAR NGG16 2-6-2+2-6-2 No.140 in red livery.

Boston Lodge works maintains the Festiniog's locomotives. *Earl of Merioneth/Iarll Meirionydd* is receiving attention to its power bogies which have been run out from under the Fairlie, which sits on accommodation bogies.

Being overhauled at Boston Lodge in August 2001 were the K1's power bogies (see page 50). When K1's overhaul is complete, the first Beyer Garratt will be sent to work on the Welsh Highland Railway.

The replica Lynton & Barnstaple 2-6-2T *Lyd* takes shape in the works. Much of the revenue from the guest driver programmes is going towards funding *Lyd*'s construction.

Boston Lodge is also responsible for the Festiniog's carriage fleet. A four wheel 'bug-box' is seen in the middle of a complete re-build.

Some work is contracted out, the repairs to *Merddin Emrys'* boiler being one such example. The boiler was sent to Israel Newtons in Bradford for repair, compare this view with that on page 32.

Less glamorous but equally significant is the Heritage Lottery-funded restoration of a rake of slate wagons. Two of the slate wagons are in the works receiving attention.

The Festiniog has a diverse and historically important collection of passenger coaches. Stabled in the sidings at Harbour station are two 'bug-boxes' Nos 5 and 6, together with two bowsiders, the nearest being No.20 of 1879.

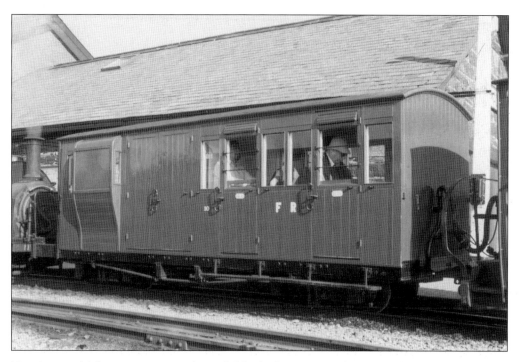

No.10 started life in 1873 as a curly-roofed brake luggage van (see page 9) and was re-built in 1920-1921 as a brake 3rd with matchboard sides, the condition to which it was restored in 1991.

The ex-Lynton & Barnstaple brake 3rd No.15 was bought in 1959 and re-built as a buffet car in 1963. Seen here running in 1999, the coach has been restored as closely as possible to its L&B appearance.

No.120 was built in 1980 as a three saloon/lavatory coach. As with most of the new build of coaches No.120 has aluminium side panels.

No.15, along with No.16, was built in 1872 and at the time the pair were the first true bogie coaches to run in regular service in Great Britain. Another notable first was the use of a wrought-iron frame.

Thanks to a Heritage Lottery grant Nos 15 and 16 were completely re-built. No.15 was restored to as near original condition as possible and returned to traffic in 2001. It is seen at Tan-y-Bwlch in August 2001. No.16 returned to traffic in 1930s condition in October of the same year.

Coach No.111, immediately behind *Earl of Merioneth/Iarll Meirionydd* was built in 1990 with a driver's compartment to run with the push-pull diesel locomotives. At peak time the push-pull train is used with other stock behind steam locomotives as seen here on a down train entering Portmadoc station.

Blanche's boiler certificate runs out in 2002 and it will then be a matter of conjecture as to how long she will be out of traffic. Here in August 2000 *Blanche* awaits departure from Portmadoc with a Steam & Cuisine working.

The Heritage Group's replica Minffordd down platform waiting room takes shape in August 2001 as *David Lloyd George* drifts to a halt with a Portmadoc-bound working.